Life be LIFE-ing But God be God-ing

a book of spiritual poems

DR. RENISHA HINTON

Life be LIFE-ing
But God be God-ing

a book of spiritual poems

Dr. Renisha Hinton

**LIFE BE LIFE-ING,
BUT GOD BE GOD-ING**

© 2023 THE RONTIER WHITFIELD WRITING COMPANY

All rights reserved.

No part of this publication may be reproduced, altered, stored in a retrieval system, shared, or transmitted in any form, or by any means, and for any reason - electronic, mechanical, photocopying, recording, or otherwise without the prior written consent of the copyright holder is unlawful.

Comments, questions, and requests for permission to use or reproduce materials from this publication should be directed to the author.

THE STRONG ONE

THE STRONG ONE FEELS LIKE BEING THE BIGGER PERSON,
THE BIGGER THING

YOU KNOW, THE BIGGER THING? THE RIGHT THING?

NOT REALIZING THE ATTACHMENT THAT IT BRINGS

THE ATTACHMENT OF BEING TAKEN FOR GRANTED
TO BEING OVERLOOKED

THE ATTACHMENT OF BEING CONSIDERED AS WEAK

BEING OVER-SHOOKED

THE ATTACHMENT OF FEELING LIKE YOU HAVE TO SAVE EVERYBODY

BUT WHEN YOU GO THROUGH,
WHO SAVES YOU?

THE ATTACHMENT OF TRYING TO PROVIDE FOR EVERYBODY

TRYING TO PLAY GOD, LIKE GOD AIN'T GOD

THE STRONG ONE!!!

YOU FEEL LIKE YOU THE ONE THAT GOT TO MAKE A WAY
BUT GOD IS THE ONE THAT SUPPLY EVERY NEED

BE CAUTIOUS OF THE FEELINGS, EMOTIONS,
AND TIREDNESS THAT YOU BREED

"THE BLESSINGS OF THE LORD, IT MAKETH RICH, AND ADDETH NO SORROW WITH
IT"

BUT WE SOMETIMES WANT TO BE SO STRONG, THAT WE OVER DO IT

END OF TIRED AND OVERWHELMED IN A PIT

THEN WE WANT TO BLAME GOD

AND PITCH A FIT

AS IF GOD'S WORD AIN'T THE
GUARANTEED KIT

WE ALL FALL SHORT OF HIS GLORY

WE MUST ADMIT

INCREASE YOUR RELATIONSHIP WITH
GOD

LIFE IS NO SKIT

THE REAL STRONG ONE KNOWS HOW TO RELEASE TEARS AND SUBMIT

THE WORLD WANTS US TO BELIEVE THAT BEING STRONG

MEANS SHOWING NO SIGNS OF WEAKNESS

BUT GOD'S WORD SAYS
(II CORINTHIANS 12:9-10)

"MY GRACE IS SUFFICIENT FOR YOU,
FOR MY POWER IS MADE PERFECT IN WEAKNESS

THEREFORE I TAKE PLEASURE IN INFIRMITIES

IN REPROACHES

IN NECESSITIES

IN PERSECUTIONS,

IN DISTRESSES FOR CHRIST'S SAKE

FOR WHEN I AM WEAK, THEN I AM STRONG"

THE WORLD WANTS YOU TO GET IT ALL WRONG

THEY WANT YOU TO CAST YOUR PEARLS BEFORE THE SWINE

THEY DON'T WANT YOU TO SHAKE THE DUST OFF YOUR FEET

IT'S TIME FOR THE STRONG ONE TO TAKE THE PROPER SEAT

THE PROPER SEAT OF HEALING AND NOT SACRIFICING

UNLESS GOD SAYS SO

THE PROPER SEAT OF BEING ABLE TO SAY NO

WHEN GOD TELLS YOU TO SAY NO

THE PROPER SEAT OF MOVING OUT THE WAY

SO GOD CAN HAVE HIS WAY

THE PROPER SEAT OF DOING NO MORE OR LESS THAN WHAT GOD SAYS

KNOWING THAT GOD IS THE POTTER AND YOU ARE THE CLAY

SURRENDERING TO GOD'S WILL

EACH AND EVERYDAY

UNDERSTANDING THAT SPEAKING THE WORD IS WHAT YOU SAY

DEFEATING YOUR GOLIATH

AND LETTING GOD HAVE HIS WAY

THE STRONG ONE REALLY AIN'T THAT TOUGH

BECAUSE THE STRONG ONE KNOWS

THEIR STRENGTH IS NOT ENOUGH

BE STRONG IN THE LORD

AND IN THE POWER OF HIS MIGHT

THE REAL STRONG ONE DOESN'T HAVE
TO FIGHT

THEY CAST UP ALL THEIR CARES

AND USE NO MIGHT

NO MORE BEING OVERWHELMED

NO MORE BEING DEPRESSED

NO MORE THROWING IN THE TOWEL

NO MORE BEING DOUBLE MINDED

NO MORE TAKING ASSIGNMENTS THAT'S NOT YOURS

NO MORE BEING FRUSTRATED

BECAUSE GREATER IS HE

THAT IS IN YOU

THAN HE THAT IS IN THE WORLD

SO I JUST WANT TO SAY

"HELLO"

STRONG ONE

QUESTION

WHAT DOES BEING "THE STRONG ONE" MEAN TO YOU?

THE STRONG ONE

DEAR GOD

DEAR GOD, IT'S ME

I'M WRITING TO YOU

SOMETIMES

I HAVE NO CLUE

SOMETIMES

I WISH I KNEW YOUR PLAN

SOMETIMES

I WISH I COULD SEE YOUR HAND

SOMETIMES

I WISH I COULD COMPREHEND

SO I COULD UNDERSTAND

I KNOW YOUR WORD SAYS YOU WOULD NEVER PUT MORE ON ME THAN I CAN BARE

SOMETIMES THE HURT RUNS TOO DEEP TO COMPARE

PAIN AFTER PAIN

STILL WANTING TO PLEASE YOU

WHY DO I CARE?

I WISH THE PAIN COULD BE REMOVED

LIKE HAIR IS REMOVED WIH NAIR

JUST WASHED AWAY AFTER 5 MINUTES

YET THE PAIN STAYS

AND LOOKS AT MY HEART

AND STARES

ON SO MANY LEVELS I'M TIRED

SOMETIMES

WISHING MY LIFE WAS FIRED

WISHING THAT I COULD TAKE MY LIFE

BUT I KNOW TOO MUCH ABOUT YOUR WORD

WISHING THAT JUST MAYBE SOMEONE WOULD HURT ME BECAUSE MY SPIRIT AIN'T THAT BOLD

GOD I KNOW YOU KNOW MY STRUGGLES BEST

I'M JUST TIRED

I STATED I WAS TIRED

JUST FOR MY STRENGTH TO BE REHIRED

YOU SPOKE TO ME OVER AND OVER

SAYING TO WHOM MUCH IS GIVEN

MUCH IS REQUIRED

AFTER PLEADING WITH YOU

TO LET ME COME HOME WITH YOU

I SPECIFICALLY SAID

"HOME WITH YOU"

BECAUSE I KNOW YOU HAVE A
SENSE OF HUMOR, YES YOU DO

BUT THEN JOHN 14 SAYS

"YOU KNOW HIM, FOR HE DWELLS
WITH YOU AND WILL BE IN YOU"

EITHER WAY I WAS GOING HOME WITH YOU

JUST NOT THROUGH THE CLOUDS
THAT'S SO BLUE

I REALIZED AFTER TALKING TO GOD

I HAD TO WRITE

HAD TO LET YOU ALL KNOW TO ALWAYS FIGHT

NEVER GIVE UP

TRUST IN SPITE

GOD CAN MAKE YOUR LOAD LIGHT

GOD CAN MAKE YOUR LOAD LIGHT

WALK BY FAITH AND NOT BY SIGHT

WHEN GOOD IS PRESENT

SO IS EVIL

IT'S ALSO SAFE TO SAY

WHEN EVIL IS PRESENT

SO IS GOOD

NEVER ALLOW YOUR TEST, TRIAL, AND TRIBULATIONS TO BE MISUNDERSTOOD

GOD IS ALWAYS GOOD

JOURNAL

WRITE A LETTER TO GOD

DEAR GOD

OVERCOMER

THE SUN IS SHINING AND ALL THINGS ARE GOING GOOD

SOMETIMES DARKNESS GETS THINGS MISUNDERSTOOD

WE WANT THE GREAT LIFE

WITHOUT THE MESS

BUT HOW CAN WE BECOME GREAT

WITHOUT THE TEST

WE ALL FALL SHORT OF HIS GLORY

I MUST CONFESS

GOD MAKES US STRONG EVEN WHEN WE'RE WEAK

CAN'T CONTEST

WE SERVE THE GREAT I AM

DON'T LET YOUR TESTS LEAVE YOU DEPRESSED

DELIGHT IN YOUR WEAKNESSES AND INSULTS

BECAUSE I KNOW A GOD THAT GIVES MIGHTY RESULTS

I KNOW A GOD THAT CALLED A MAN'S NAME 3 TIMES AND HE ROSE FROM THE DEAD

I KNOW A GOD THAT TOOK TWO FISH AND FIVE LOADS OF BREAD AND MADE SURE EVERYBODY WAS FED

I KNOW A GOD THAT SPLIT THE RED SEA

IKNOW A GOD THAT PUT BREATH INTO YOU AND ME

SOMETIMES WE FORGET

HOW BIG GOD REALLY IS

SOMETIMES WE FORGET HOW BIG BECAUSE WE ALLOW PEACE TO LEAVE US

ALLOW SORROW TO OVER TAKE US

ALLOW TRIBULATIONS TO BREAK US

ALLOW CHAINS TO HOLD US

ALLOW GENERATIONAL CURSES TO FOLLOW US

YET, WE HAVE A MIGHTY GOD THAT IS STILL AVAILABLE

AVAILABLE TO HEAL US

AVAILABLE TO DELIVER US

AVAILABLE TO TRANSFORM US

AVAILABLE TO UNLOCK US

AVAILABLE TO PUSH US

AVAILABLE TO PROSPER US

WE HAVE TO UNDERSTAND HOW GOOD GOD REALLY IS

IF YOU DON'T UNDERSTAND

I WILL UNDERSTAND FOR YOU

I WOULDN'T BE HERE IF GOD DIDN'T PULL ME THROUGH

GOD GAVE ME ANSWERS WHEN I DIDN'T KNOW WHAT TO DO

PLENTY OF TIMES HE HAD TO PICK ME UP

WHEN I JUST WANTED TO LAY DOWN

MANY TIMES HE HAD TO

READJUST THIS QUEEN'S CROWN

THROUGH ALL THE HEARTBREAKS AND DISAPPOINTMENTS

GOD STILL COMFORTED MY HEART

GOD KEPT ME

FAVORED ME

GRACED ME

IN SPIRIT OF MY FALSE STARTS

THE WORLD GAVE ME EVERY REASON TO BE BITTER

BECAUSE OF HEARTBREAK

MOLESTATION

DECEIT

BUT HOLD ON

LET ME PUT MY PRAISES TO GOD ON REPEAT

GOD I THANK YOU FOR KEEPING ME

I THANK YOU FOR NOT LETTING DIVORCE BREAK ME

I THANK YOU FOR NOT LETTING
SUICIDAL THOUGHTS OVERTAKE ME

I THANK YOU FOR COMFORTING ME

I THANK YOU FOR UPLIFTING ME

I THANK YOU FOR YOUR SPIRIT

WHEN FLESH WANTED TO BREAK FREE

I THANK YOU FOR KEEPING MY BUSINESSES

IN SPITE OF WHAT'S GOING ON

I THANK YOU FOR THE STRENGTH TO REMAIN STRONG

YOU ALLOWED ME TO OVERCOME HER

BECAUSE I AM AN OVERCOMER

QUESTION

WHAT HAS GOD ALLOWED YOU TO
OVERCOME WHEN YOU THOUGHT
YOU COULDN'T?

OVERCOMER

HIS CHILD

MY FATHER IS A FATHER
THAT TOOK MY BIOLOGICAL FATHER'S PLACE

WITHOUT HESITATION HE SIGNED UP FOR SOMETHING THAT WASN'T EVEN HIS RACE

TO ME THAT MEANT THE WORLD

IF IT WASN'T FOR HIM I WOULDN'T HAVE KNOWN

WHAT IT FELT LIKE TO BE DADDY'S LITTLE GIRL

MY FATHER AND MOTHER DEPARTED

HE DID WHAT WAS BEST

BUT I WAS STILL LEFT BROKEN HEARTED

HE CAME TO PICK ME UP ALMOST EVERY WEEKEND

BUT EVERY WEEKEND FELT LIKE EVERYDAY

I DIDN'T WANT TO END

HE KNEW WHAT I WAS GOING THROUGH AT HOME

BUT IT WAS OUT OF HIS CONTROL

HE ALWAYS KNEW HOW TO WARM MY HEART

WHEN MY HEART FELT COLD

HE WAS ALWAYS A PHONE CALL AWAY

WHEN THINGS GOT HARD HE ALWAYS KNEW WHAT TO SAY

HE USED TO ALWAYS SAY " NENE ITS GONE BE OK"

GOD ALWAYS MADE A WAY

AND TROUBLES DON'T LAST ALWAYS

GROWING UP I DIDN'T UNDERSTAND THOSE WORDS

BUT I CAN TELL YOU THE TRUTH WAS BEING TOLD

WHEN GOD HAS HIS HANDS ON YOU

THE DEVIL BEGINS TO FOLD

TODAY I AM A LIVING TESTIMONY OF A FATHER STANDING IN A GAP OF A FATHERLESS CHILD

HE LOVES ME LIKE I AM HIS

SO EACH MOMENT MAKES ME SMILE

HE STEPPED IN

SO I'M NO STEP CHILD

HE INTRODUCED ME AND MY SISTERS AS HIS DAUGHTERS

AND TOLD US TO ALWAYS STICK TOGETHER

I TRIED TO

NO MATTER THE RESULTS OF A DNA TEST OR A LAWYER

DAD SUPPORTED ME

MORE THAN MY BIOLOGICAL MOTHER AND FATHER

YOU ALWAYS BEEN THERE

THE LOVE HE HAS SHOWN ME

BLOOD CANT COMPARE

I DON'T TAKE HIS LOVE AND SUPPORT MILD

I AM BLESSED TO BE CALLED HIS CHILD

QUESTION

HOW DO YOU KNOW YOU'RE GOD'S CHILD? HOW DOES HE CARE FOR YOU?

HIS CHILD

A SPECIAL DAY

A DAY WAS DEDICATED FOR ME

GOD HAS A BETTER PLACE FOR ME

YOU SEE

A PLACE OF NO PAIN

BETRAYAL

OR MISERY

AS IM NOT WITH YOU PHYSICALLY

I ASK YOU TO EMBRACE MY LOVE MENTALLY

REMEMBER THE GOOD TIMES

AND LOVING WORDS WE SHARED

REMEMBER AS A FATHER, GRANDFATHER, BROTHER, SON,

UNCLE, COUSIN, AND FRIEND, I ALWAYS CARED

WHEN I LOOK DOWN ON YOU

I WANT TO SEE YOU SMILE

FEEL MY LOVE FROM A MILLION MILES

WHEN YOU THINK OF ME

THINK OF SWEET SWEET VICTORY

THINK OF HOW STRONG I WAS

AND THE SMILES I PUT ON YOUR FACE

KNOW THAT I AM COVERED BY GOD'S GRACE

IRAN MY RACE AND MADE MY PEACE

WHEN YOU READ PSALMS 23

THINK OF ME

ONE DAY WE ALL WILL MEET AGAIN AND HAVE SO MUCH TO SAY

I WANT YOU TO KNOW THE DAY I LEFT TO GO WITH GOD

WAS A SPECIAL DAY

JOURNAL

RECALL ONE OF THE MOST SPECIAL
DAYS THAT GOD HAS ALLOWED
YOU TO SEE

A SPECIAL DAY

I SHALL NOT FEAR

WE SHALL NOT FEAR

WHO AM I TO SAY I GO THROUGH TOO MUCH?

I MUST STAY FOCUSED AND ACKNOWLEDGE HIS EVERY TOUCH

WHO AM I TO SAY I'M NOT BUILT FOR THIS?

KNOWING THAT GOD CREATED ME

AND THAT HE COULD GIVE THE TABLE A TWIST

WHO AM I NOT TO ANSWER WHEN HE CALLS?

KNOWING HE'S THERE TO CATCH ME BEFORE EVERY FALL

I CAN TELL YOU "GOD IS GOOD" ALL DAY LONG

BUT I MUST ALSO TELL YOU

DURING THE FIGHT YOU MUST STAY STRONG

BATTLES WILL COME LEFT AND RIGHT

STRUGGLE AFTER STRUGGLE

FIGHT AFTER FIGHT

YOUR LIFE MAY TURN FROM SWEET TO SOUR

YOU MAY HAVE TO PRAY EVERY HOUR ON THE HOUR

SOMETIMES IT'S HARD TO GET GOING

BECAUSE THE GOING GETS HARD

BUT CAST ALL YOUR CARES UNTO THE LORD

NO TEMPTATION HAS OVERTAKEN YOU THAT IS NOT COMMON TO MAN

GOD HAS ALREADY GIVEN YOU THE VICTORY TO STAND

WHEN YOU FEEL LOW AND YOU DON'T KNOW WHAT TO DO

REMEMBER GOD'S WORD SAYS

"MY GRACE IS SUFFICIENT FOR YOU"

(2 CORINTHIANS 12:9)

NO MATTER WHAT THE SITUATION LOOKS LIKE

DO NOT ALLOW YOUR FAITH TO BE WEAKENED

AND CAUSE YOUR BLESSINGS TO BE ON STRIKE

SOMETIMES YOU MAY BE SO WEAK

AND FEEL THAT PRAYER IS NOT YOUR BEST FRIEND

BUT KNOW THAT GOD WROTE THE BEGINNING AND THE END

REMEMBER THERE'S NOTHING NEW UNDER THE SUN

YOU ARE A WARRIOR

FEAR NONE

GOD POWER IS MADE PERFECT IN WEAKNESS

DONT ALLOW YOUR FAITH TO BE SLEEPLESS

THE LORD IS OUR STRENGTH AND SHIELD

BY HIS STRIPES WE ARE HEALED

TRUST GOD AND NOT BE AFRAID

GOD WILL UPHOLD YOU WITH HIS RIGHTEOUS RIGHT HAND

BE NOT DISMAYED

FORGET THE STUMPS IN THE ROAD

AND THE THIEVES IN THE NIGHT

GOD CAN MAKE YOUR FEET LIKE A DEER

AND ENABLE YOU TO GO TO HIGHER HEIGHTS

GOD IS ALWAYS HERE

FAR AND NEAR

WE SHALL NOT FEAR

QUESTION

WHAT IS YOUR BIGGEST FEAR? ARE
YOU WILLING TO RELEASE IT? WHY
OR WHY NOT?

I SHALL NOT FEAR

LOOKING AT LIFE

THERE'S DIFFERENT WAYS TO LOOK AT THE LIFE WE LIVE

BUT OUR PRIORITY SHOULD BE

TO MAKE SURE OUR PURPOSE IS FULFILLED

THERE MAY BE UPS AND DOWNS

BUT THE WAY GOD IS SET UP

HE CAN TURN EVERYTHING AROUND

WE CAN LOOK AT THINGS AS A BLESSING OR A CURSE

EVERYTHING ISN'T DESIGNED TO BE GOOD BEFORE IT GETS WORSE

SOMETIMES YOUR STRENGTH HAS TO BE BUILT UP

IN ORDER FOR YOU TO STAND

PUT YOUR TRUST IN GOD'S HAND

THERE'S DIFFERENT WAYS TO LOOK AT THE LIFE WE LIVE

WE ALWAYS WANT

BUT ARE WE WILLING TO GIVE?

ARE WE WILLING TO DO WHAT GOD WANTS US TO DO?

ARE WE WILLING TO GO THROUGH WHAT GOD WANTS US TO GO THROUGH?

WE HAVE TO LOOK AT OUR "GOING THROUGH"

AS A " STEPPING INTO"

STEPPING INTO HEALING

ABUNDANCE

UNDERSTANDING

AND PROSPERITY

STEPPING INTO GOD'S PATH IS NOT THE PATH TO POPULARITY

WE HAVE TO LOOK AT OUR DOWNFALLS AS A STEPPING STONE

DOWNFALLS ARE MEANT TO TEACH US

NOT BREAK OUR BONES

REJOICE IN YOUR HARD TIMES

UPLIFT YOUR CHEEKBONES

FOR BETTER OR WORSE

WE ARE BLESSED AND NOT CURSED

QUESTION

WHAT WAS YOUR OUTLOOK ON
LIFE FIVE YEARS AGO? HOW HAS IT
CHANGED TODAY?

LOOKING AT LIFE

NEW CREATION

THE GRASS WILL BE GREEN AND THE SKY WILL BE BLUE

THERE COMES A TIME WHEN YOU HAVE TO BE

OUT WITH THE OLD

AND IN WITH THE NEW

IN LIFE YOU WILL GO THROUGH
SOME THINGS YOU HAVE TO

ACKNOWLEDGE DARKNESS

IN ORDER TO REALIZE WHAT LIGHT WILL BRING

TESTS, TRIALS, AND TRIBULATIONS CAN BUILD YOU

GIVING THE DEVIL THE GLORY WILL
DELAY YOUR BREAKTHROUGH

THE WORLD WILL DECEIVE YOU BUT GOD WILL UPLIFT YOU

IGNORE THE WORLD'S EVERY WORD

AND LISTEN TO GOD'S EVERY CLUE

A WORLDLY WOMAN DOESN'T REALIZE
THE BENEFIT OF BREAKTHROUGH

NOR THE BENEFIT OF THE STRENGTH
FROM THE THINGS WE GO THROUGH

NOR THE USELESS EXTRA ROUTES THAT WE TRAVELED

DOING WHAT WE WANTED TO DO

THE DARKNESS OVER YOUR LIFE

WILL MAKE YOU FEEL LONELY AT TIMES

BUT ACCEPT THE LIGHT OF JESUS

AND ALLOW YOUR WORLD TO SHINE

GOD SAID

"COME TO ME ALL YOU WHO ARE WEARY
AND BURDENED AND I WILL GIVE YOU REST"

YES HE CAN GIVE U REST

NO MATTER HOW LONG OR COMPLEX THE TEST

GOD IS THE ANSWER TO ALL

YOU MAY SOMETIMES FEEL LOW

BUT HE CAN CATCH YOU RIGHT BEFORE YOUR WORLD FALLS

NOT KNOWING YOUR WORTH AS THE WOMAN
GOD HAS CREATED YOU TO BE

WILL HAVE YOU PLAYING A PART IN ADULTERY

WILL HAVE YOU THINKING SIMPLE

AS IF HE DIDN'T CREATE YOU TO BE EXTRAORDINARY

WILL HAVE YOU WANTING TO END YOUR LIFE

AS IF GOD DIDN'T ALREADY GIVE YOU THE VICTORY

TO HANDLE ANY STRIFE

WILL HAVE YOU QUESTIONING GOD

BECAUSE SOMETHING DIDN'T GO

THE WAY YOU WANTED IT TO

IGNORING THE FACT

GOD'S GOT YOUR BEST INTEREST AT HEART

IN ALL YOU GO THROUGH

NOT KNOWING YOUR WORTH AS A WOMAN

AND CHILD OF GOD

WILL HAVE YOU THINKING LOW OF YOURSELF

AS IF GOD DIDN'T SAY YOU ARE ALTOGETHER BEAUTIFUL

MY LOVE

THERE IS NO FLAW IN YOU

WHEN YOU ARE TIRED OF DARKNESS

ALLOW THE LIGHT TO SHINE THROUGH

KNOW THAT YOU ARE PRICELESS

WORTH MORE THAN RUBIES

KNOW THAT YOU CAN NOT BE BOUGHT

WITH MONEY

SWAG

REPUTATION

JEWELRY

THE LOVE THAT GOD HAS FOR YOU IS NO MYSTERY

KNOW THAT GOD CAN GIVE YOU YOUR HEART DESIRES

KNOW THAT NOTHING IS TOO HARD

AND THE DEVIL IS A LIAR

LET US HOLD FAST THE PROFESSION
OF OUR FAITH WITHOUT WAVERING
JESUS IS IN THE BUSINESS OF SAVING

GOD SAID GIVE ME YOUR HEART
AND LET YOUR EYES DELIGHT IN MY WAYS,

ALLOW GOD TO LIGHT YOUR PATH AND NOT GO ASTRAY

AND YOU WERE DEAD IN YOUR TRESPASSES AND SINS

FOR YOU HAVE BEEN BORN AGAIN

NOT OF SEED WHICH IS PERISHABLE BUT IMPERISHABLE

YOU ARE A CREATION OF SHE

YOU CAN BE WHO GOD CREATED YOU TO BE

ALLOW GOD TO DIRECT YOUR LIFE

ORDER YOUR STEPS AND CHANGE YOUR STATION

YOU ARE A NEW CREATION

QUESTION

WHAT HAS GOD CHANGED ABOUT
YOU THAT YOU NEVER THOUGHT
COULD CHANGE?

NEW CREATION

GOD KNOWS

TESTS

TRIALS

TRIBULATIONS

READ IT ALL IN REVELATIONS

WE FACE NEW BATTLES EVERYDAY

NO NEED TO WORRY

JESUS IS ALL YOU HAVE TO SAY

WHEN YOU THINK YOU GOT IT BAD

SOMEONE ELSE GOT IT WORSE

YOU HAVE TO BREAK EVERY CHAIN

DESTROY EVERY CURSE

YOU HAVE TO

PRAY

READ

FAST

GOD'S WORD WILL FOREVER LAST

REGARDLESS OF THE SITUATION

YOU MUST STAND

YOU MUST BELIEVE YOU HAVE THE BEST GOD AT HAND

YOU WERE CREATED FROM DUST

NOT SAND

YOU CAN'T BE WATERED DOWN

BOUNCE BACK LIKE A RUBBER BAND

YOU ARE GOD'S CHILD

NO MATTER WHAT IS SAID BY MAN

MAN MAY RENT OUT PROPERTY

DEUTERONOMY 1:8

GOD HAS ALREADY GIVEN YOU LAND

YOU HAVE NOT BECAUSE YOU ASK NOT

GOD GAVE UP HIS SON FOR YOU

HAVE YOU FORGOT?

YOU CANNOT LET SITUATIONS DESTROY YOU

BECAUSE GOD CREATED YOU

WALK THE WALK GOD HAS PAVED FOR YOU

DO WHAT YOU GOT TO DO

GOD IS THE ANSWER TO ALL

IF YOU ONLY KNEW

WHEN YOU'RE FALLING APART

ALLOW GOD TO BE THAT GLUE

YOUR SEASON WILL ARRIVE WHEN IT IS DUE

FOLLOW GOD

THE WORLD ONLY WANTS TO STREW

THERE ARE SOME THAT HAVE LOST LOVE ONES

BUT YOU HAVE TO LET GOD'S WILL BE DONE

LET YOUR PAST BE YOUR PAST

MATTHEW 20:16

THE LAST WILL BE FIRST

AND THE FIRST WILL BE LAST

SOME HAVE BEEN MISUSED AND BEAT

SOME BEEN LEFT FOR DEAD IN THE STREET

SOME BEEN CALLED EVERY NAME

EXCEPT A CHILD OF GOD

SOME BEEN STOLEN FROM

FROM SOCKS TO IPODS

SOME BEEN CHEATED ON

NEGLECTED

BUT GOD'S GOT YOU

SO LET IT ALL BE RESPECTED

SOME BEEN LIED TO AND DECEIVED

BY GOD'S GRACE

YOU WERE RELIEVED

SOME OF US WERE MOLESTED OR RAPED

WASN'T BELIEVED BECAUSE IT WAS TOO LATE
FOR THE EVIDENCE TO BE SCRAPED

BUT GOD CREATED A MENTAL ESCAPE

SOME BEEN PUT OUT OF HOMES

HAD NO MONEY FOR BILLS

BUT WITH PRAYER

YOUR REQUEST WILL BE FULFILLED

SOME HAD TO DO JOBS

THAT THEY DIDN'T WANT TO DO

WHEN YOU TRUST GOD

HE WILL BRING YOU THROUGH SOME TOUGH TIMES

HAD TO SLEEP IN CARS AND DANCE AT BARS

BUT GOD CAN HEAL ALL WOUNDS AND SCARS

SOME PEOPLE BEEN TURNED ON

SO THEY TURNED ON DEPRESSION

THROUGH IT ALL

LET GOD BE YOUR MAIN LESSON

SOME PEOPLE HAVE HAD FAILED MARRIAGES

NO MARRIAGES, FAKE MARRIAGES

SOME HAD IT ALL

IF THE FOUNDATION AIN'T GOD

IT WILL FALL

WE ALL HAVE BEEN THROUGH IN LIFE

BUT LET NO SITUATION BOUND YOU

THINK TWICE

CRY EVERY TEAR, PRAY EVERY PRAYER

JUST KNOW YOU NOT ALONE

BECAUSE GOD KNOWS

QUESTION

EVEN THOUGH GOD KNOWS, WHAT DO YOU WANT TO EXPRESS TO GOD ON TODAY? GOD LOVES FOR US TO BE REAL WITH HIM.
DID YOU KNOW THAT WHAT YOU RELEASE INTO THE ATMOSPHERE CAN BREAK CHAINS?

GOD KNOWS

OH, HOW HE LOVES ME

GROWING UP I DIDN'T KNOW I WAS BLESSED

DIDN'T FEEL LIKE I WAS THE QUEEN OF CHESS

FELT MORE LIKE THE TARGET OF DODGE BALL

AS IF I WAS CREATED TO FALL

I REMEMBER MY FATHER TELLING ME

"NEENEE GOD GOT YOU

IT WILL BE BETTER DAYS"

I WOULD RESPOND "BUT WHEN, DADDY?"

BECAUSE MY STRUGGLES WERE ON REPEAT

AND MY LIFE WAS A MAZE

ATTACK AFTER ATTACK

MOLESTED TIME AFTER TIME

WHILE SLEEPING ON MY BACK

NEVER GOT WHIPPING

I ALWAYS GOT BEATINGS

I WAS ALMOST GIVEN AWAY FOR DRUGS

LIKE IT WAS TRICK OR TREATING

DIDN'T KNOW WHAT IT FELT LIKE TO BE IN A STATIONARY SCHOOL

BECAUSE I WENT TO ALMOST EVERY ELEMENTARY SCHOOL

DIDN'T HAVE ANYONE TO HELP ME WITH MY HOMEWORK

ALWAYS MADE A'S AND B'S THOUGH

GOD CREATED NO FOOL

OH HOW HE LOVES ME

DIDN'T UNDERSTAND WHY I ALWAYS WANTED TO BRING IN NEW YEARS IN CHURCH, BUT CLUBBED AFTER SERVICE

MANY DIDN'T UNDERSTAND, BUT IT WAS THE BEGINNING OF MY PROCESS OF FULFILLING MY PURPOSE

OH HOW HE LOVES ME

I USE TO STUTTER AND HAVE STAGE FRIGHT

DON'T GET ME WRONG, I STILL GET BUTTERFLIES

AND MY STOMACH STILL GETS TIGHT

IF YOU WOULD HAVE TOLD ME SEVEN YEARS AGO

I WOULD BE WHERE I AM TODAY

I WOULD HAVE SHOOK MY HEAD AND SAID "NO WAY"

IF YOU WOULD HAVE TOLD ME

I HAD TO TALK BACK WITH AUTHORITY

AND LAUGH AT THE DEVIL LIKE HE LAUGHS AT ME

I WOULD HAVE LOOKED AT YOU LIKE "ARE YOU CRAZY?!"

I REMEMBER MY PASTOR TELLING ME

I AM A CHOSEN ONE AND HIGHLY FAVORED

AS I SEEK GOD MORE I REALIZE

TESTS, TRIALS, AND TRIBULATIONS ARE CUSTOM-TAILORED

FOR I KNOW THE PLANS I HAVE FOR YOU, DECLARES
THE LORD, PLANS TO PROSPER YOU AND NOT TO HARM YOU,
PLANS TO GIVE YOU HOPE AND A FUTURE

(JEREMIAH 29:11)

I NO LONGER FELT LIKE I WAS BEING

STITCHED TOGETHER WITH SUTURES

OH HOW HE LOVES ME

I USED TO NOT UNDERSTAND WHY I ALWAYS GAVE
PEOPLE THE BENEFIT OF A DOUBT AND WHY I HAD A BIG HEART

THEN, GOD REVEALED TO ME THAT
FORGIVING IS THE BEGINNING OF A NEW START

I DIDN'T UNDERSTAND HOW I COULD GO
THROUGH SO MUCH AND FEEL UNBOTHERED

I THOUGHT IT WAS ABNORMAL

BUT GOD REVEALED THAT
HIS PEACE IS VERY FORMAL

OH, HOW HE LOVES ME

MY BODY WAS AT THREAT OF CANCER

WAITING A MONTH AND HALF TO GET TESTED

FOR RESULTS I CLAIMED HEALING AND TOLD THE DEVIL
HE WOULD HAVE NO LUCK

I WROTE THIS WHOLE POEM ON
SEVERAL OCCASIONS BETWEEN THE
HOURS OF 1AM AND 4AM

AFTER THE FIRST 2 OCCASIONS, I WANTED TO
WRITE MORE AND MORE

OH, HOW HE LOVES ME

GOD IS MY STRENGTH WHEN I'M WEAK

HE ANSWERS WHEN I SEEK

HE WIPES MY TEARS WHEN I CRY

HE REMINDS ME OF MY FUTURE WHEN I THINK I WANT TO DIE

HE SOFTENS MY HEART WHEN I WANT IT TO BE HARD

HE RENEWS MERCY EVERYDAY WITH A FRESH START

OH, HOW HE LOVES ME!

OH, HOW HE LOVES ME!

OH, HOW HE LOVES ME!

HE HAS ENOUGH LOVE FOR US ALL

WE JUST HAVE TO SURRENDER ALL

GOD'S LOVE IS UNCONDITIONAL FOR US

THERE'S NO DEBATE TO DISCUSS

OH, HOW HE LOVES US

QUESTION

GOD LOVES YOU. HOW MUCH
DO YOU LOVE GOD? WHAT ARE
YOU WILLING TO DO?

OH, HOW HE LOVES ME

GOD KNEW YOU WOULD TELL

THE KITCHEN SOMETIMES GET HOT

AND TIMES GET HARD

ALWAYS TRY YOUR BEST

TO KEEP GOD'S PEOPLE FROM FALLING APART

DAYS GOT LONGER

MONEY GETS SHORTER

NEVER ALLOWED YOUR PRAISE TO BECOME DISTORTED

NEVER GIVE IN TO THE ENEMIES ATTACKS

MISSION ABORT

I LIKE TO SAY WELCOME TO THE FIGHT

WE KNOW WARFARE IS MORE THAN A SPORT

GOD'S WORD TEACHES US WAYS TO FIGHT

THE ENEMY IS ON THE HOME COURT

REGARDLESS OF THE FOUNDATION OF THE BUILDING

KEEP FAITH THAT GOD CAN RENEW IT

REGARDLESS OF THE ENEMIES WORD ATTACKS

YOU DIDN'T ALLOW IT TO MAKE YOU HAVE A FIT

REGARDLESS OF THE SLEEPY NIGHTS

TEARY EYES

STAY FOCUSED ON THE GOLDEN PRIZE

YOU KNOW GOD'S REWARD

IS THE GREATEST OF ALL

YOUR FAITH IS DETERMINED NOT TO LET
GOD'S HOUSE FALL

GOD KNEW YOU WOULD NOT ALLOW HIS
MISSION TO FAIL

GODS KNOWS HIS WORD

YOU WOULD FOREVER TELL

QUESTION

WHAT ARE YOU WILLING TO EXPOSE
TO ENSURE THAT GOD GETS THE
GLORY?

GOD KNEW YOU WOULD TELL

GOD'S TIMING

SOMETIMES THE KITCHEN GETS HOT

TIMES GET HARD

ALWAYS TRY YOUR BEST TO KEEP
GOD'S PEOPLE FROM FALLING APART

DAYS GOT LONGER

MONEY GETS SHORTER

NEVER ALLOWED YOUR PRAISE
TO BECOME DISTORTED

NEVER GIVE IN TO THE ENEMY'S ATTACKS

"MISSION ABORT"

WELCOME TO THE FIGHT

WE KNOW WARFARE IS MORE THAN A SPORT

GOD'S WORD TEACHES US WAYS
TO FIGHT THE ENEMY ON THE HOME COURT

REGARDLESS OF THE FOUNDATION OF THE BUILDING

KEEP FAITH THAT GOD CAN RENEW IT

REGARDLESS OF THE ENEMY'S WORD ATTACKS

YOU DIDN'T ALLOW IT TO MAKE YOU HAVE A FIT

REGARDLESS OF THE SLEEPY NIGHTS AND TEARY EYES

YOU STAYED FOCUS ON THE GOLDEN PRIZE

YOU KNOW GOD'S REWARD IS THE GREATEST OF ALL

YOUR FAITH IS DETERMINED NOT TO LET GOD'S HOUSE FALL

GOD KNEW YOU WOULD NOT ALLOW HIS MISSION TO FAIL

GODS KNOWS HIS WORD

YOU WOULD FOREVER TELL

QUESTION

HOW PATIENT ARE YOU WITH GOD'S TIME? WILL YOU TRUST HIM REGARDLESS OF HOW LONG IT TAKES?

GOD'S TIMING

LIFE BE LIFE-ING, BUT GOD BE GOD-ING

LIFE KNOWS HOW TO FLIP YOU UPSIDE DOWN

MAKE YOU THINK TWICE

AND FORCE YOU TO READJUST YOUR CROWN

THE ENEMY OFFERS SNACKS

CONTAINING MOMENTS OF PLEASURE

GOD OFFERS FULL COURSE MEALS

THAT CONTAIN HIDDEN TREASURES

LIFE SOMETIMES HITS

SLAPS

KICKS

I'M HERE TO DELIVER THE ALREADY KNOWN TRICK

GOD HAS GIVEN YOU THE STRENGTH

TO MOVE EVERY MOUNTAIN

HE HAS PROVIDED AN EVERLASTING FOUNTAIN

YOU DON'T HAVE TO BOW TO THE TACTICS OF THE ENEMY

YOUR WELL DOESN'T HAVE TO RUN DRY

HE REPLIED,

"BECAUSE YOU HAVE SO LITTLE FAITH.

TRULY I TELL YOU, IF YOU HAVE FAITH

AS SMALL AS A MUSTARD SEED,

YOU CAN SAY TO THIS MOUNTAIN,

'MOVE FROM HERE TO THERE, AND IT WILL MOVE.

NOTHING WILL BE IMPOSSIBLE FOR YOU."

MATTHEW 17:20

SEE, NOTHING IS IMPOSSIBLE FOR YOU

YOU HAVE THE AUTHORITY, YES YOU DO

ATTACKS MAY HAPPEN BACK TO BACK

YOU DON'T HAVE TIME TO CUT THE ENEMY NO SLACK

CRY OUT TO GOD

AND WIPE THOSE TEARS

GOD DELIVERS IN THE TIMES OF TROUBLE

HE HEARS

GEAR UP AND TAKE AUTHORITY

FAITH OR FEAR IS YOUR PRIORITY???

"FINALLY, BE STRONG IN THE LORD

AND IN HIS MIGHTY POWER.

PUT ON THE FULL ARMOR OF GOD

SO THAT YOU CAN TAKE YOUR STAND

AGAINST THE DEVIL'S SCHEMES

FOR OUR STRUGGLE IS NOT AGAINST FLESH AND BLOOD

BUT AGAINST THE RULERS

AGAINST THE AUTHORITIES

AGAINST THE POWERS OF THIS DARK WORLD

AND AGAINST THE SPIRITUAL FORCES OF EVIL IN THE HEAVENLY REALMS

"THEREFORE PUT ON THE FULL ARMOR OF GOD
SO THAT WHEN THE DAY OF EVIL COMES
YOU MAY BE ABLE TO STAND YOUR GROUND
AND AFTER YOU HAVE DONE EVERYTHING TO STAND
STAND FIRM
THEN WITH THE BELT OF TRUTH BUCKLED AROUND YOUR WAIST
WITH THE BREASTPLATE OF RIGHTEOUSNESS IN PLACE
AND WITH YOUR FEET FITTED WITH THE READINESS
THAT COMES FROM THE GOSPEL OF PEACE
IN ADDITION TO ALL THIS, TAKE UP THE SHIELD OF FAITH
WITH WHICH YOU CAN EXTINGUISH
ALL THE FLAMING ARROWS OF THE EVIL ONE
TAKE THE HELMET OF SALVATION AND THE SWORD OF THE SPIRIT
WHICH IS THE WORD OF GOD. AND PRAY IN THE SPIRIT
ON ALL OCCASIONS WITH ALL KINDS OF PRAYERS AND REQUEST
WITH THIS IN MIND
BE ALERT AND ALWAYS KEEP ON PRAYING FOR ALL THE LORD'S PEOPLE."
EPHESIANS 6:10-18
YOU GOT THIS
I PRAY YOUR LIFE NEVER BE THE SAME
AND THAT YOU BE STRONGER THAN YOU EVER BEEN
I DECLARE, DECREE, AND BELIEVE THAT NO MOUNTAIN IS STRONGER
THAN THE GOD IN YOU
ARMOR UP AND LET'S GO
LIFE BE LIFE-ING, BUT GOD BE GOD-ING

QUESTION

WHAT WAS ONE OF THE HARDEST
LICKS YOU TOOK IN LIFE? HOW DID
GOD RESTORE YOU?

LIFE BE LIFE-ING, BUT GOD BE GOD-ING

WHICH WAY

WITHOUT NOTICE, YOU EVER CAUGHT YOURSELF WONDERING?

MIND GOING 100 MILES PER HOUR

HEART JUST POUNDING

YOU SEEMS LOST

YOU LOOKING UP

YOU LOOKING DOWN

NOTHING IS MAKING SENSE

NO SMILE

JUST A FROWN

IT SEEMS AS IF THE WORLD IS CLOSING IN ON YOU

YOU THINKING AND YOU THINKING

BUT NOT KNOWING WHAT TO DO

EVERY TIME YOU FIND THE STRENGTH TO RISE

THE ENEMY POPS UP

SURPRISE

YOU ALLOW HIM TO TEAR APART YOUR HEART

PUT YOU 4 STEPS BEHIND THE START

YOU ALLOWED THE ENEMY TO ENTER YOUR MIND

AND INTERROGATE YOUR THOUGHTS

YOU WAS SO MUCH INTO FLESH

YOU FORGOT TO REALIZE

ALL YOU HAD TO DO WAS PRAY TO POP'S

NEVER ALLOW THE ENEMY TO COME INTO YOUR HOME

AND DESTROY WHAT GOD CREATED

BECAUSE GOD'S WORD IS SO

AND WILL FOREVER BE

IT CAN NEVER BE REINVENTED TO BE RESTATED

THE STRENGTH OF THE DEVIL IS OVERRATED

WE ALLOW THE ATTACKS OF THE DEVIL TO BE OVERWEIGHTED

WE ALLOW THE DEVIL TO FILL OUR LIFE WITH SO MUCH MESS

BRINGING UP OUR PAST

WHEN WE KNOW ALL WE HAVE TO DO IS CONFESS

THE ENEMY WANT US TO TURN AWAY FROM GOD WHEN WE HAVE A TRIAL, TRIBULATION, OR TEST

WE SOMETIMES ALLOW THE ENEMY TO SIT ON OUR SHOULDER

LIKE A LIL PEST

PLAYING WITH US LIKE WE'RE AT RECESS

I'M HERE TO TELL YOU NO MORE WONDERING

BECAUSE GOD GOT US FROM THE NORTH, SOUTH, EAST AND WEST

WE DONT HAVE TO BE CURSED

BECAUSE WE ARE BLESSED

WE ARE THE HEAD, NOT THE TAIL

CHOOSE GOD AND YOU WILL NOT FAIL

CHOOSE HEAVEN AND NOT HELL

WHAT IS DEATH WHEN GOD SAID HE GIVES YOU LIFE

GOD GIVES US THE OPTION OF CHOICE

THINK TWICE

NO NEED TO STRESS

JUST THINK

NO NEED TO WONDER

DONT EVEN BLINK

NO MORE WONDERING WHICH WAY

NO MORE GOING ASTRAY

NO MORE WONDERING WHICH WAY

JESUS IS NOT ONLY THE TRUTH AND THE LIGHT

BUT ALSO THE WAY

NO MORE WONDERING WHICH WAY

NO MORE ASKING WHICH WAY

JESUS IS THE WAY

QUESTION

WHICH WAY ARE YOU
WILLING TO GO?

WHICH WAY

FAITH

FAITH

BEING SURE OF WHAT WE HOPE FOR

AND CERTAIN OF WHAT WE DO NOT SEE

CLAIMING THINGS AS IT ALREADY BE

FAITH IS THE ASSURANCE THAT GOD'S PROMISES WILL NEVER FAIL

EVEN WHEN YOU ARE DOWN AND OUT

DOWNING WITHOUT A SAIL

FAITH IS SAYING "GOD I TRUST YOU"

EVEN WHEN YOUR SITUATIONS SAY YOU CAN'T

FAITH IS MOVING WHEN GOD TELLS YOU TO MOVE

WHILE FEELING LIKE YOU ARE NOT READY

WE MUST REMEMBER GOD IS ALWAYS ON POINT AND STEADY

TIMES GET HARD AND FAITH MAY NOT BE YOUR BEST FRIEND

KEEP IN MIND THAT GOD HAS THE LAST SAY SO IN THE END

IT GETS SO TOUGH THAT SOMETIMES YOU THROW IN THE TOWEL

BUT WE SERVE A GOD THAT THROWS THE TOWEL BACK AT YOU

GOD SAYS "LET'S WIN"

THE ENEMY KNOWS HOW MUCH HAVING FAITH MEANS TO GOD

THAT'S WHY HE ATTACKS IT

NO MATTER WHAT

YOU HAVE GOT TO TAKE THE HIT

"AND WITHOUT FAITH IT IS IMPOSSIBLE TO PLEASE GOD

BECAUSE ANYONE WHO COMES TO HIM

MUST BELIEVE THAT HE EXISTS

AND THAT HE REWARDS THOSE WHO EARNESTLY SEEK HIM"

HEBREWS 11:6

"THAT YOUR FAITH SHOULD NOT STAND IN THE WISDOM OF MEN

BUT IN THE POWER OF GOD"

1 CORINTHIANS 2:5

MAY YOUR FAITH BE INCREASED IN THIS SEASON

LIKE NEVER BEFORE

I DECLARE AND DECREE THAT YOU WILL BELIEVE

ABOVE YOUR OWN ABILITY

AMEN

QUESTION

HOW STRONG IS YOUR FAITH? ARE YOU WILLING TO LET GOD INCREASE YOUR FAITH REGARDLESS OF HOW CRAZY YOU MAY LOOK?

FAITH

JOURNAL

USE THESE EXTRA PAGES TO WRITE
DOWN YOUR DREAMS, DESIRES,
PRAYERS, AND DAY-TO-DAY
REVELATIONS FROM GOD